Benji
~Little Bear's Underwear Scare~
アクティビティブック

できたね！シール

できたね！

できたね！

できたね！

できたね！

できたね！

できたね！

できたね！

できたね！

できたね！

できたね！

できたね！

できたね！

できたね！

できたね！

よびシール

じぶんのすきな
できたね！シールを
つくろう

Benji
~Little Bear's Underwear Scare~

アクティビティブック

Activity Book

Written by
**Patricia Daly Oe
Mari Nakamura**

······················· はじめに ·······················

お休みの日に外に遊びに行きたいクマのベンジー。でも、みんな忙しくてなかなか一緒にお出かけできません。やっとおじさんが一緒にお出かけしてくれることになりますが、またもや困ったことに！ さて、ベンジーは遊びに行けるでしょうか？ 繰り返しが多くて覚えやすいストーリーと楽しいアクティビティで、家族の名前やお家やお外ですぐに使えるフレーズを学びましょう。

Benji the little bear wants to play outside, but he can't find anyone to play with. Finally he finds his uncle, who loves to play outside. But his uncle says Benji cannot go outside. Why is that? With a fun story and lots of language repetition, this activity book lets children learn many expressions that they can use at home and outside.

mpi

もくじ  Table of contents

アクティビティブックについて

このアクティビティブックは
絵本 **Benji** ~Little Bear's Underwear Scare~（別売り）に対応しています。
アクティブ・ラーニングの概念に沿った「学ぶ」「考える」「創作する」「遊ぶ」の
4つのカテゴリーで英語力と思考力、クリエイティビティ、協調性を育みます。

This activity book is based on the picture book "Benji ~Little Bear's Underwear Scare~".
The activities in the four active learning categories of "learning", "thinking", "creating" and "playing" foster
abilities in English language, thinking, creativity and collaboration through observation, word puzzles,
chants, stickers, simple crafts and games.

ことばをまなぼう
Let's Learn

絵本に出てくる単語や関連する新しいことばをチャンツ、シール貼り、線結びなどを通して学びます。ここで楽しく身につけた語彙力が次からの活動の基礎となります。

かんがえよう
Let's Think

仲間分けや身近な場所、身の回りを観察するアクティビティを通して思考力を養います。答えが決まっていない活動は、子どもの自主性や自由な発想も養います。

つくろう
Let's Create

色塗りやシンプルな工作に取り組み、出来上がったものを英語で表現します。その過程で子どもは、創意工夫する喜びや表現する楽しさを経験し、創造力を身につけていきます。

あそぼう
Let's Play

ごっこあそびやボードゲームを通して、想像力や協調性を養います。また、これまでに習った英語を遊びを通して使うことにより「英語ができる！」という自信を育みます。

アクティビティブックの効果的な使い方

1. まず、対応の絵本、DVDでストーリーを楽しみましょう。そのあとにこのアクティビティブックに取り組むと、学習効果がアップします。

2. アクティビティは、一度にたくさん進めるよりも、少しずつ楽しみながら取り組んでいきましょう。上手にできたら できたね！シール を貼って、ほめてあげましょう。

3. このアクティビティブックの4〜5ページ、10〜11ページのチャンツはアプリで聴けますので、繰り返し聞いて英語の音やリズムを体で覚えていきましょう。（アプリの使い方は、24ページをご覧ください。）

指導者の方へ
教室では、一人一人の個性的な表現を尊重し、違いを認め合う雰囲気で活動を進めましょう。生徒が絵や作品について日本語で話した時は、それを英語に直して語りかけたり、その英語をリピートするように促したりして、英語を話せるように導きます。

保護者の方へ
絵本の世界を味わいながら、ゆったりとした気分で進めていきましょう。この本には、子どもの自由な表現を促す、答えが決まっていない活動も多く含まれています。💡取り組みのヒントを参考に、子どもと一緒に伸び伸びと英語の探索を楽しみましょう。

えじてん
Picture dictionary

チャンツのリズムにのって、
たんごをいいましょう。
Chant the words.

えじてんのえカード（p.27-29）で
あそびましょう。
Play with the picture cards on pages twenty-seven to twenty-nine.

♪ スマートフォンをかざして
チャンツをききましょう
Listen to the chant with a smart phone.

▲ チャンツで、たんごをいいましょう。
　Chant the words.

▲ チャンツで、たんごとぶんをいいましょう。
　Chant the words and sentences.

できたね！
シール
sticker

1 school

2 outside

3 play

4 underwear

5 mom

6 dad

7 uncle

8 aunt

Benji

9 sister

10 brother

11  cook

 I'm cooking.

 12  dress

 I'm dressing.

 13  do my homework

 I'm doing my homework.

 14  watch TV

 I'm watching TV.

 15  fix the car

 I'm fixing the car.

 16  play the guitar

 I'm playing the guitar.

シールをはろう
Fun with stickers

なににつかうものかかんがえて、シールをはりましょう。
Find and place the stickers.

できたね！
シール
sticker

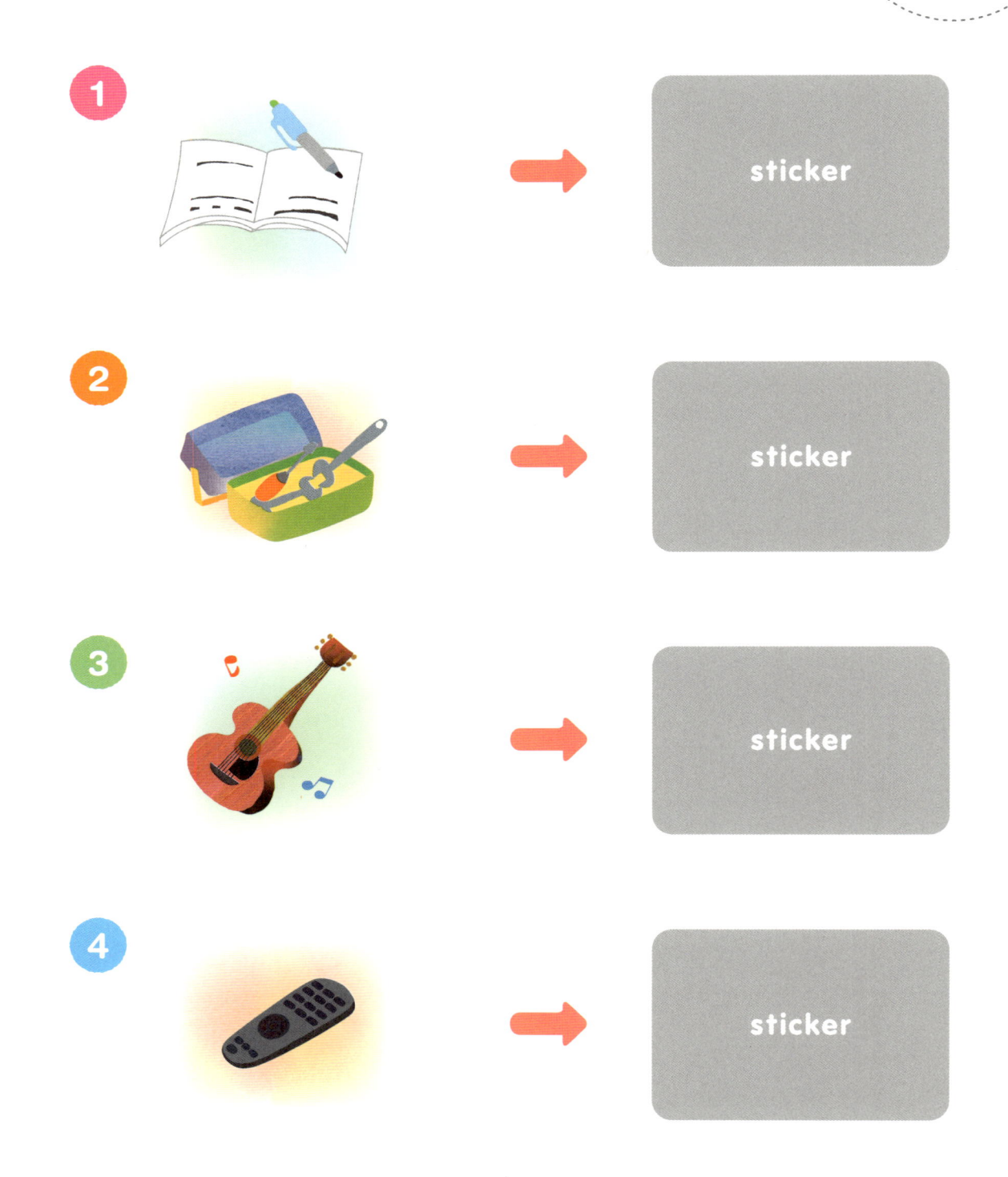

1 → sticker

2 → sticker

3 → sticker

4 → sticker

取り組み
のヒント
Learning Tips

シールを貼る時には、一緒に英語を言ってみましょう。
Say the words together as children put the stickers in place.

6

さがそう
Search for the pictures

だれのものかな？
えほんをみてさがして □ にばんごうをかいて、かぞくのことばをなぞろう。
Find and write the numbers in the □ . Then trace the words.

- - - - - - - - - - ✏ なぞる

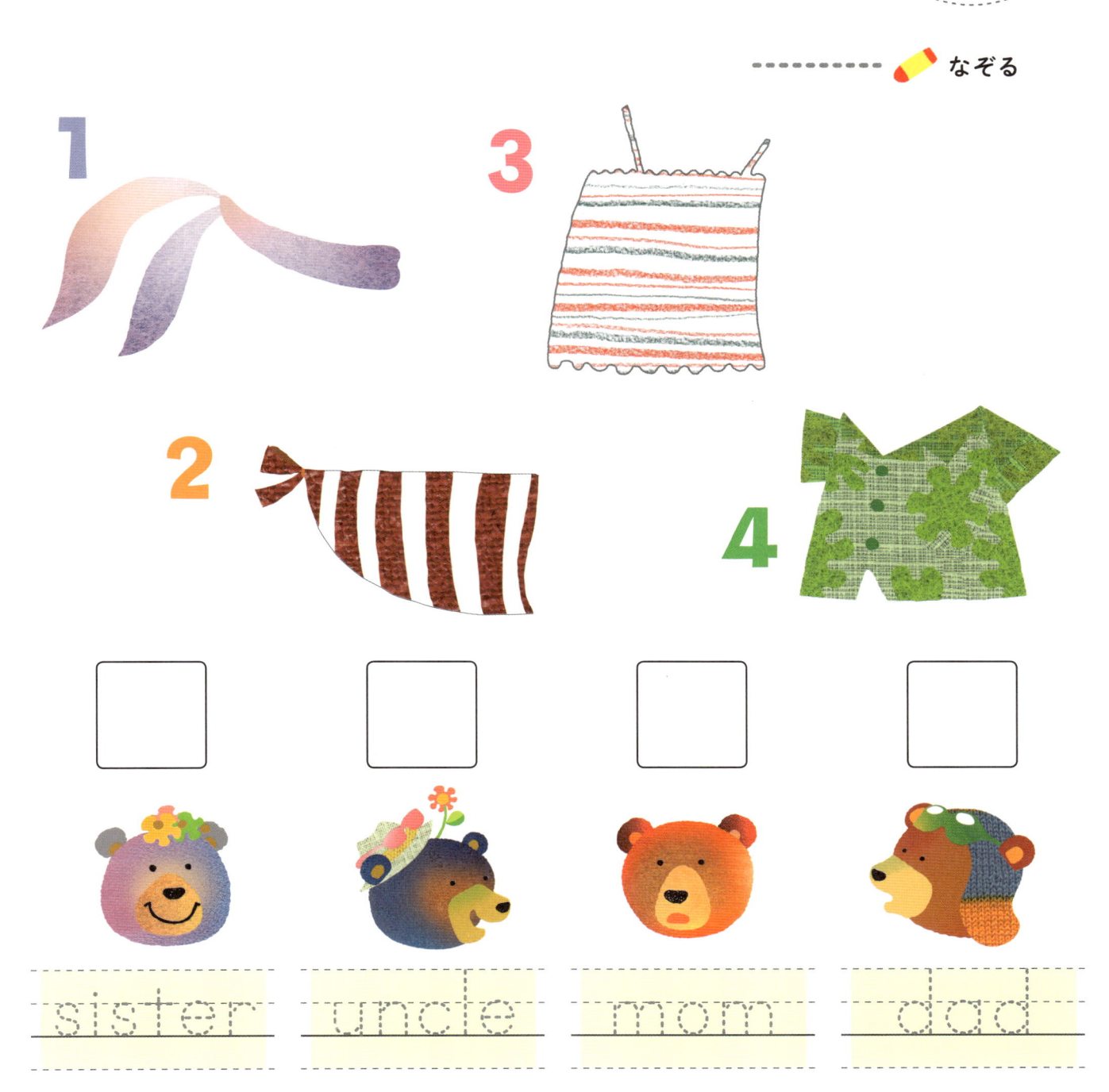

1

2

3

4

sister   uncle   mom   dad

**取り組み
のヒント**
Learning Tips

まず、絵本を見ずに答えを書いてみて、そのあと絵本を見ながら答え合わせをしましょう。家族のことば
は言いながら書きましょう。衣服のことば（apron、scarf、shirt、underwear）も言えるといいですね。

First of all, try and think of the answers without looking at the picture book. Check with the
pictures in the picture book afterwards. Say the words for the family members when writing the
words and try and say the words for the clothes (apron, scarf, shirt, and underwear), too.

なぞろう
Trace letters

えいごをいってなぞりましょう。
Say the words and trace.

- - - - - - - - - - 🖍 なぞる

aunt

dress

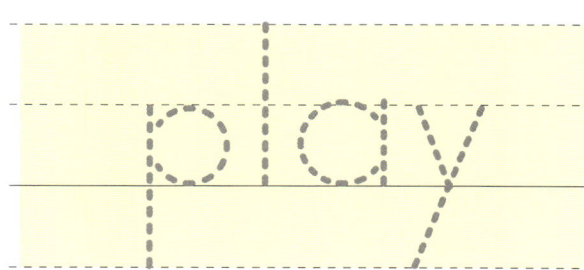

play

outside

取り組み
のヒント
Learning Tips

なぞる前となぞった後に、英語を言ってみましょう。
Say the words in English before and after tracing them.

せんでむすんでなぞろう
Connect with lines and trace

えとえいごをせんでむすび、もじをなぞりましょう。
Connect the picture with the word and trace.

⬛---------⬛ ✏ なぞる

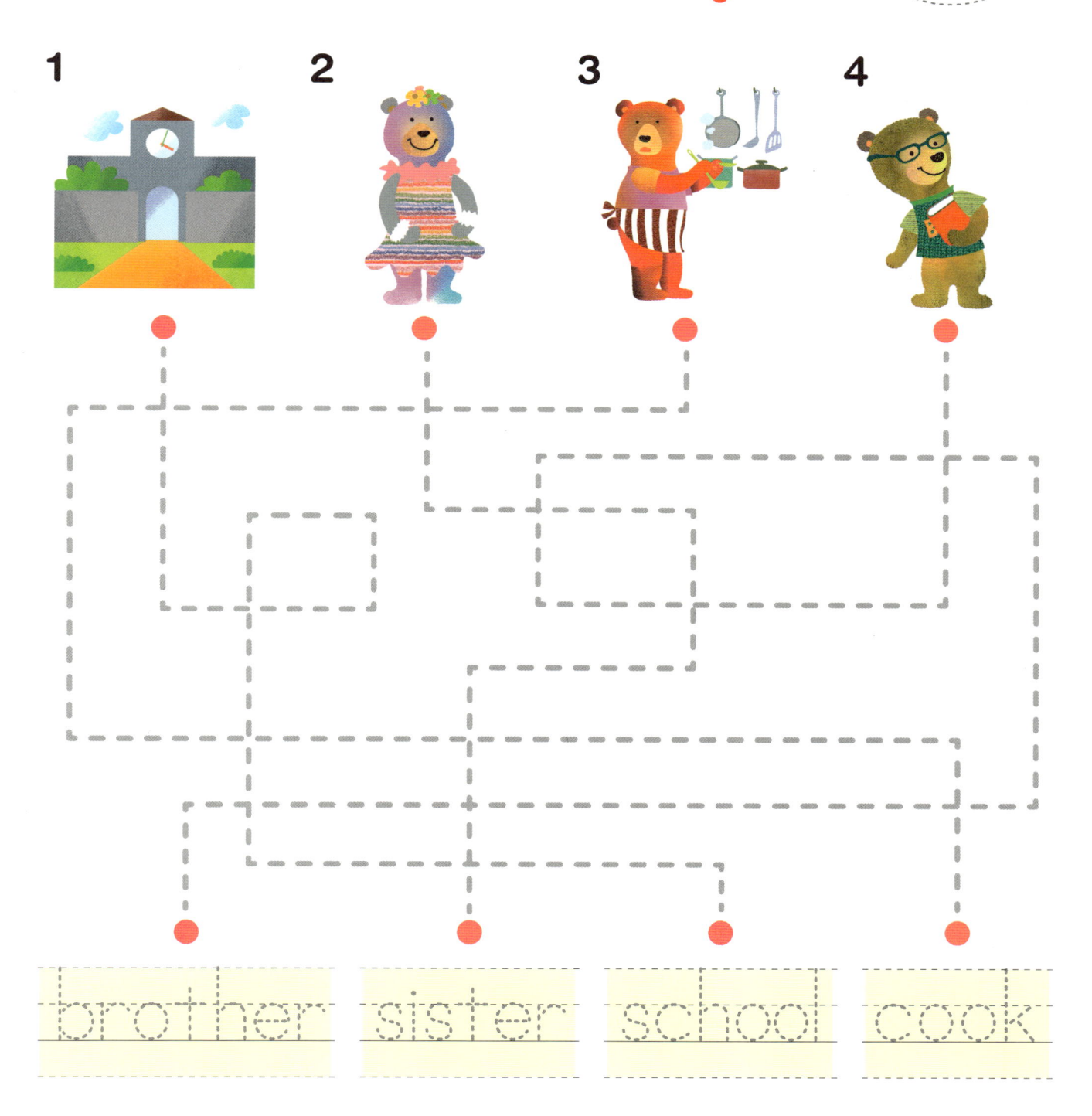

1　**2**　**3**　**4**

brother　sister　school　cook

取り組み
のヒント
Learning Tips

英語を読めない子どもには、読んであげましょう。
Please read the words to children who cannot read.

あたらしい ことばを おぼえよう

Learn more words

あたらしい ことばの  スマートフォンをかざして チャンツをききましょう

Listen to the chant with a smart phone.

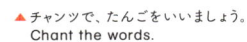

▲ チャンツで、たんごをいいましょう。
Chant the words.

▲ チャンツで、たんごとぶんをいいましょう。
Chant the words and sentences.

できたね！
シール
sticker

ほかにどんなことばがあるかな？
シールをはって、えカード（p.27-31）であそびましょう。

Find and place the stickers. Play a game with
the picture cards on pages twenty-seven to thirty-one.

1

school

park

supermarket

2

cook

wash

clean

3

watch TV

draw pictures

listen to music

④

fix the car   water the plants   take out the trash

⑤

play the guitar   **play soccer**   **play tag**

⑥

do my homework   **read a book**   **exercise**

取り組み のヒント
Learning Tips

絵本に出てこない身近なことばを練習してみましょう。それぞれどんな仲間でしょうか。新しい単語はチャンツで聴くことができます。27〜31ページに絵カードがありますので、一人が単語を言って、もう一人がカードを取るような遊びをしてみましょう。

Let's practice some other words related to the words in the story. How are they connected? You can listen to the chants for pronunciation. You can use the picture cards on pages 27 to 31 to play a simple game where one person says a word and the other person finds the matching card.

なにかな？

What is it?

Br にちゃいろ、Bl にあお、R にあか、Y にきいろをぬりましょう。
ギターのうしろにはだれがかくれているかな？
ぬけているもじをかいて、たんごをかんせいさせましょう。
ヒントはしたにあるよ。
Br＝brown　Bl＝blue　R＝red　Y＝yellow
What's hiding behind the guitar?
Choose the words from the Hints and write the letters.

Br ＝brown　Bl＝blue　R＝red　Y＝yellow

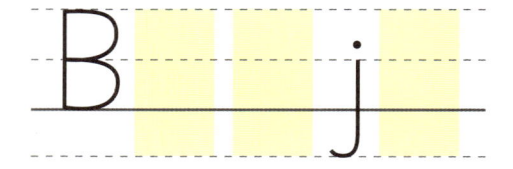

B＿＿j

Hints　Beth　Benji　Amy
Harry　Mike

**取り組み
のヒント**
Learning Tips

指示通りに色を塗ると、絵本のキャラクターが出てきます。絵が出てきたら、ヒントを参考に単語を完成させ、言ってみましょう。

When the parts of the picture are colored in as indicated, a character is revealed. Say what it is together. Write the letters.

みつけてなぞろう
Find and trace

Benji のかぞくは、なにをしているかな？
あうえいごをえらび □ に ○ をつけ、もじをなぞりましょう。
What are Benji's family doing?
Find the correct sentence, mark it with a circle in the □
and then trace the words.

できたね！
シール
sticker

---------------- ✏ なぞる

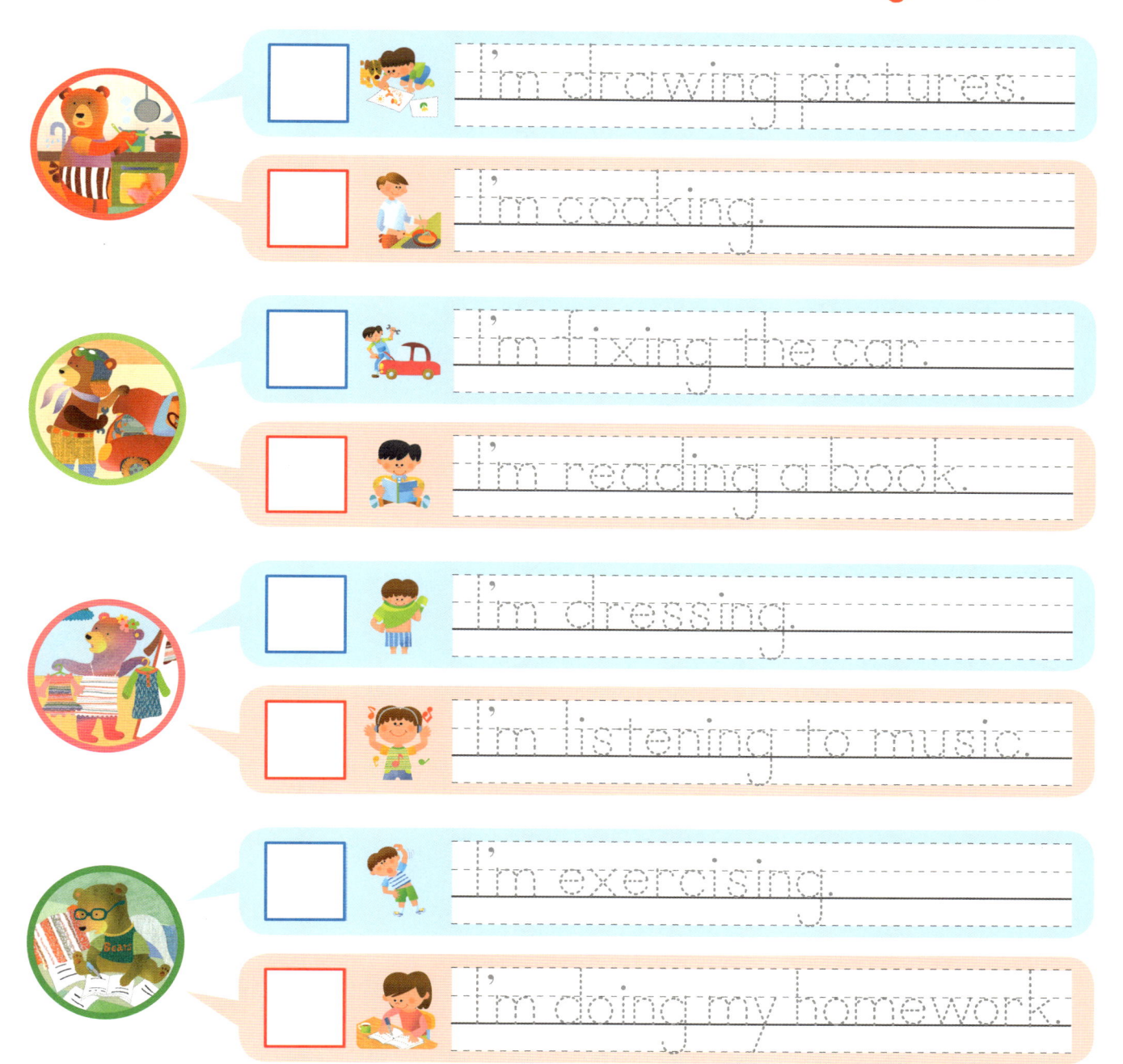

I'm drawing pictures.

I'm cooking.

I'm fixing the car.

I'm reading a book.

I'm dressing.

I'm listening to music.

I'm exercising.

I'm doing my homework.

わけてみよう

Put into groups

えをゆびさしてえいごをいってみましょう。
Point and say the words.

みんなは、どんなことをおうちやそとでするかな？
おうちですることと、そとですることにわけて、みぎのページにえをかきましょう。
そして、じぶんがすきなことのえもかきましょう。

Do you do these things at home or outside?
Draw the pictures on the next page.
Then draw a picture of something you like to do.

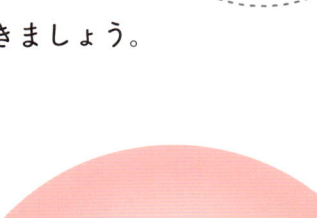

do my homework

water the plants

play soccer

watch TV

exercise

draw pictures

play tag

read a book

● おうちですること
At home

● そとですること
Outside

● なにをするのがすき？
What do you like to do?

**取り組み
のヒント**
Learning Tips

答えは一人一人違うかもしれませんね。子どもの考えを尊重しましょう。絵は、例えば play soccer だったらサッカーボールだけ描いても構いません。好きなことについては I like to play soccer. のように言えるといいですね。

Children may differ in their answers and drawings and it is important to respect the child's free expression. It is fine if a child wants just to draw a soccer ball for "play soccer." When answering what they like to do, it would be good, for example, if the child is able to say "I like to play soccer."

よくみてかこう
Look and find

みんなのかぞくは、おやすみのひにどんなことをするかな？
10〜11ページの ②〜⑥ からさがして、えをかきましょう。

What do you and your family do in your free time?
Look at the phrases on pages ten and eleven, and draw the pictures.

取り組み
のヒント
Learning Tips

10〜11ページの動詞・動詞句の中から、家族が休日にすることを選んで絵を描きます。絵は簡単で構いません。Who's watching TV? などと、描いた絵について質問をしてみましょう。

Look at the pictures of activities on pages 10 to 11 and choose which of them you and other members of your family do in your free time. Children can ask and answer questions about their pictures, for example, "Who's watching TV?"

ぬりえをしよう
Enjoy coloring

すきないろでぬりましょう。
Color the picture.

できたね！
シール
sticker

**取り組み
のヒント**
Learning Tips

色を塗ったら、英語で言えるものを一緒に探して言ってみましょう。

After children have colored in the picture, search for words together that they can say in English.

つくろう

Create your own picture

Benji と Benji のおねえちゃんに、ようふくをきせよう。
みぎのページにあるようふくやぼうしなどをきってはりましょう。

Dress up Benji and his sister.
Make the design by choosing the items from the next page.
Cut and paste.

**取り組み
のヒント**
Learning Tips

19ページの絵を切り離して、このページに並べて貼って、Benji と Benji のおねえちゃんに洋服を着せて
あげましょう。yellow shirt のように英語で言ってみましょう。

Cut out the items on page 19 and dress Benji and his sister. Try to use English. for example.
"Yellow shirt."

8 cut きる

ごっこあそびをしよう
Role-playing

えをみてまねをしましょう。
Look at the pictures and practice.
したのえではおとこのこになって、あそびにいけない
りゆうをかんがえて ＿＿＿＿＿ にいれていってみましょう。
Think why the boy cannot go outside and play, and write the reason on the line.

できたね！
シール
sticker

Can we go outside and play?

Sure!

Can we go outside and play?

Sorry, I'm very busy.

I'm ＿＿＿＿＿＿＿＿＿.

取り組み
のヒント
Learning Tips

応用として、おもちゃ、ぬいぐるみを使って、同様の会話を練習してみましょう。
Practice the same kinds of conversations by using toys or stuffed animals.

ボードゲームをしよう
Play a board game

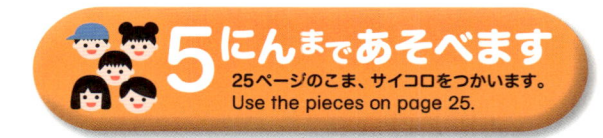5にんまであそべます
25ページのこま、サイコロをつかいます。
Use the pieces on page 25.

Benjiといっしょにこうえんにあそびにいくすごろくゲームです。
・じゅんばんにサイコロをふって、サイコロのかずだけすすみます。
・どうさのえのマスにとまったら、そのどうさをしながら I'm <u>cooking</u>. や I'm <u>watching TV</u>. の
　ようにいいます。
・🦁 にとまったら、Yippee-yippee-yay! といって、もういちどサイコロをふることができます。
・🦁 にとまったら、Oh, no! といって、いっかいおやすみです。
・いちばんはやくこうえんにたどりついたひとがかちです！

- Roll the dice in turn. Go forward the number of spaces shown on the dice.
- When you land on a space with an action word and phrase, say "I'm <u>cooking</u>." while doing the action.
- If you land on a space with Benji, say "Yippee-yippee-yay!" roll the dice again and move forward.
- If you land on a space with a pair of torn underpants, miss a turn and say "Oh, no!"
- The winner is the person who gets to the goal the fastest.

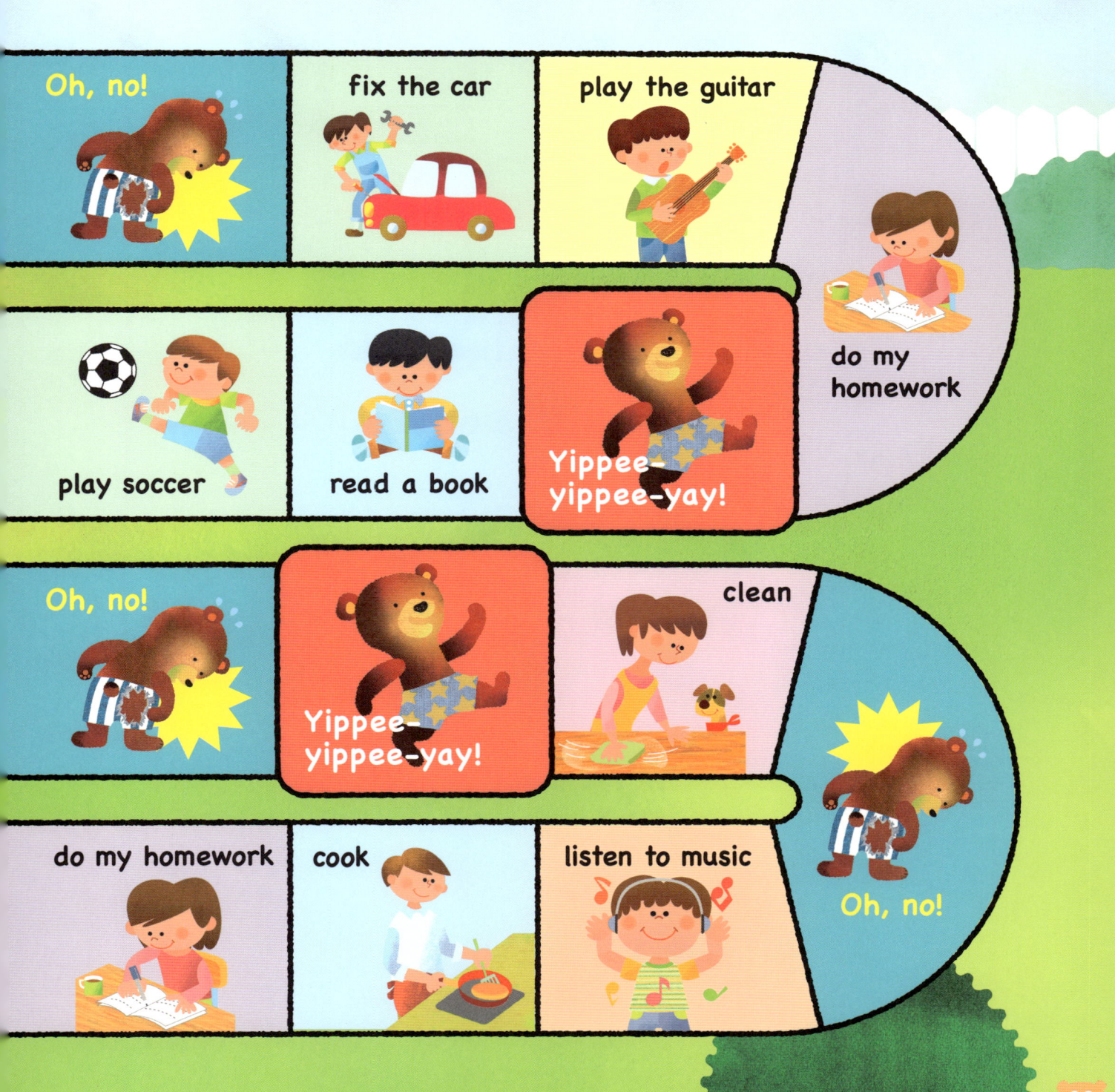

アプリの使い方

スマートフォンをかざしてチャンツをききましょう　あたらしいことばのスマートフォンをかざしてチャンツをききましょう　のページ（p.4-5、10-11）では、英語の音声を聴くことができます。

以下の方法で、お手持ちのスマートフォンやタブレットにアプリ（無料）をダウンロードしてご使用ください。

アプリダウンロード方法

オトキコ

お持ちのスマートフォンやタブレットで下記のQRコードを読み込んでください。
※ QRコードリーダーをインストールされている方

iphone、iPadをお使いの方

Android端末をお使いの方

または

AppStore／Googleplayで検索の枠に『mpi オトキコ』と入力して検索をしてください。　

●著者紹介

Patricia Daly Oe（大江パトリシア）

イギリス、ケント州出身。日本の英語教育に従事するかたわら、数多くの紙芝居と絵本を創作。著書に『Peter the Lonely Pineapple』『Blue Mouse, Yellow Mouse』『Lily and the Moon』などがある。英会話を教えていて、英語の先生のためのワークショップを開催しながら、ナレーションの活動や子供のイベントなどもしている。

Patricia Daly Oe is a British picture book author and teacher who also enjoys giving presentations. and holding events for children.

公式ホームページ ● http://www.patricia-oe.com

中村 麻里

金沢市にて英会話教室イングリッシュ・スクエアを主宰。幼児から高校生の英語指導にあたるかたわら英語教材、絵本の執筆、全国での講演にたずさわり、主体性や表現力など21世紀型スキルを伸ばす指導法の普及につとめている。イギリス・アストン大学TEYL〔Teaching English to Young Learners〕学科修士課程修了。2013年 JALT学会 Best of JALT（ベスト・プレゼンター賞）受賞。

Mari Nakamura is a school owner, teacher trainer and ELT materials writer who loves good stories and playing with children.

公式ホームページ ● http://www.crossroad.jp/es/

Benji ～Little Bear's Underwear Scare～
アクティビティブック

発行日	2017年9月27日　初版第1刷
	2021年10月4日　初版第3刷

執　筆	Patricia Daly Oe / Mari Nakamura
イラスト	イケベ ヨシアキ
デザイン	柿沼 みさと、島田 絵里子
協　力	mpi English School 本部校
英文校正	Glenn McDougall
編　集	株式会社 カルチャー・プロ
音　楽	株式会社 Jailhouse Music
プロデュース	橋本 寛
録　音	株式会社 パワーハウス
ナレーション	Rumiko Varnes
印　刷	シナノ印刷株式会社
発　行	株式会社mpi 松香フォニックス
	〒151-0053
	東京都渋谷区代々木2-16-2 第二甲田ビル2F
	fax 03-5302-1652
	URL　https://www.mpi-j.co.jp/

[22〜23ページ ボードゲーム] クマのこま、サイコロをきりはなしましょう。

● こま markers

glue　　　glue　　　glue　　　glue

------- cut きる
glue はる
------- fold やまおり

● サイコロ
dice

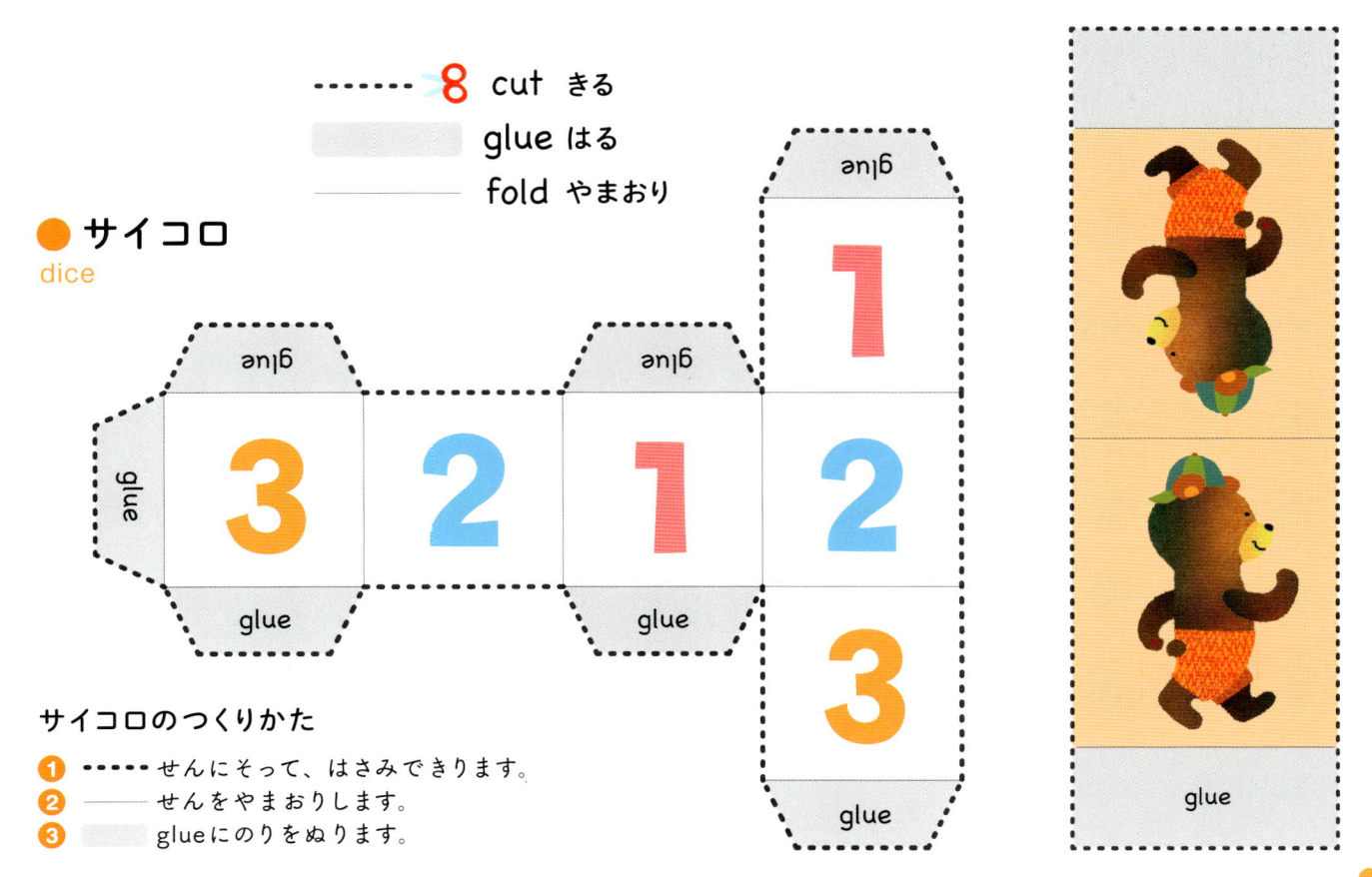

glue

glue　　glue　　1

3　2　1　2

3

glue　　glue

サイコロのつくりかた

① -------- せんにそって、はさみできります。
② ———— せんをやまおりします。
③ glueにのりをぬります。

glue

[4〜5/10〜11ページ　えカード]
ごうけい30まい（よび2まい）

Picture cards for pages 4-5 and 10-11
30 cards (with 2 extras)

-------------- ✂ cut きる

school

outside

play

underwear

mom

dad

uncle

aunt

sister

brother 	cook 	dress 
do my homework	watch TV	fix the car 
play the guitar 	park 	supermarket 
wash 	clean 	draw pictures 

listen to music	water the plants	take out the trash

play soccer	play tag	read a book

exercise